TURN THE PAGE OVER BEFORE DIVING HEADSFIRST

ZIQR PEEHU

Made with ♥ on the Notion Press Platform
www.notionpress.com

for saj-dah

Contents

Contents

Contents

Preface

Acknowledgements

Living and dreaming are perpendicular. And at the point of intersection I do something I hadn't thought of. I walk into your arms.

-@spensert4933 on a youtube comment

Elliptical Disenfranchisement of Memory

Though, you're gone

Almost unimaginable

Other than the reality of it

All and the page remains

Still. You're not here to turn it

Over. I cannot save myself

Loving you was an unreliable saviour

Being loved -

Unreliable.

Me - in your arms. Me - in love. Me - warmth.

You - call at 1AM. You - sleep to an insomniac by virtue of existence.

I let the evening catapult

Itself into night like I'm okay

With change. Ignore - that you're here.

Ignore - I'm okay with anything if you're here.

Thud - your heartbeat - Thud - you don't know why it's beating

This fast. I can't help myself.

Memory is a reliable saviour.

Elliptical messiah. A memory starts where

A memory ends. Me in your arms.

Me in love. Me warmth. I ask you to

Locate the north star and you only

Look at me. Question - What is a saviour?

Answer - silence. Answer - A look.

I morse code words in a language you don't know.

You don't let me go. The memory loops over.

Me - in your arms. Me - in love. Me - Warmth.

You whisper love you - This breaks the spell.

You leave. Memory - a broken cassette.

Memory - Hammer to a mirror. Memory - franchised existence.

No one turns the page over. I don't die yet.

Faiz.

The gods have a silent promise. Three wishes

Across a life time and sometimes you beg your way into one of
them

But sometimes they throw it unexpectedly on an August morning

I imagine God's office as a year long exercise in desi bureaucracy

Like a long attempt in patience in waiting in hoping.

A blue jay snares his wing before an attempt at survival.

I think of all the things we'd do to live.

You're a boy - eclipsing - the moon - the tidal waves - tired
metaphor - teen boy beyond ideas of love & longing - labelled
light on a jar - hollow between an awakening.

When I think of God - now, I imagine him standing next to you

Always, a little to the side sitting in on a feast. Divinity is an
exercise in trying

But mostly in loving

So - of course, you're there.

Being strong is a flimsy flight towards testimonials - towards natural selection - towards

You'd be here a hundred years from now but you make it sound more holy

Your existence - like a chapel in a hospital

One foot here and the other with God.

You make it sound like the fight comes before the flight but that both are important

Blue jay tired metaphor fights his way into existence before flying always.

Desi Child Discovers this Thing Called Strength

Hanuman didn't know the extents of his own strength or his weakness so his mother was often heard encouraging him with sentences like "You can uproot the mountain" but "Don't swallow the sun"

I am a young boy and

I've been learning. Often the error

Is a Missed word. Or Misrepresented.

I fear I've angered the gods but

Uncle Sun says I'm okay. He'll forgive me at

The risk of his reputation

Because amusement out does

Anger. No one tried to eat the

Damn Sun-

Stop. A mouth slapped on his face as he looks up. Damnation doesn't count when he starts the day but

There are worse punishments than being a seven headed snake but

the thunder doesn't hit and

Uncle Dad doesn't storm off into oblivion so

We Move Past It

Mother says I'm beyond death

When I was born. No one died. A stillness of shadow on

A moving day. The grim reacher touched no one to

Celebrate me. If I die it's going to be for

Reasons beyond strength.

I once flew across nations to

Prove my worth but mostly

To

Be

Loved.

These days when

I'm a young boy

I calculate the trajectory

Of my will and

End up some place where

I'm revered.

These days. Mother is dead so I

Lift everything and eat more but

My holiness was borne of love.

The only place beyond me is

Heaven.

We are all looking for love. I stitch my chest back up. Proof is
beyond the living.

I'd Love You On A Ferry Between The Diomede Islands

What I mean is how deeply fortunate a life

Heard by angels, lived twice.

I asked for love and got the day twice

In return. What I mean is, I want to listen to

Your Monday morning blues after I'm done

Suffering through mine so I can listen without

Interruption and only Sympathy and how you

Drive with a single hand to look cool but when

You're tired, both hands on the wheel and how I

Want to experience you buckling my seatbelt in

Twice each weekend before you forget your worry

For someone you know seeing you. I want to make

You forget twice, each moment. I want to celebrate

Your birthday twice and underline a different gift on

My calendar for each one because my brain

Doesn't shut up about things to get you because

You ask me for the world and I almost

Become a capitalist to buy it for you.

What I mean is, I want to wish on four 11:11's a day for

You because only something half this miraculous

Could fit you being in my life. So I could outline your face with

Sunrise twice a day and not regret capturing the light badly

The first time around when you distract me. What I mean is, I get your jokes

The first time around but I laugh harder on the second go.

Because it takes you a day to read half a book so I want

To give you a day that is two days so you could say

It took you a day to finish the book. What I mean is,

I love you across geographical metaphors and time illusions

What I mean is, one time around isn't enough.

Give me twice. If you'd let me. I'd love you on a

Ferry between the Diomede Islands. I'd love you twice

In a single lifetime.

The Other Woman

Dreamt last night I fed you, unknowingly, something you were

allergic to.

and you were gone, like that.

You don't have even a single allergy, but still. The dream cracked.
Cars nose-dived

off snow banks into side streets. Sometimes dreams slip poison,
make the living

dead then alive again, twirling in an unfamiliar room.

It's hard to say *I need you* enough.

Dreamt this morning I set you up, knowingly, arrogantly

and you were gone, like that.

You don't even like her but still. The dream cracked. The limbo
world-scape

Folded in on itself crushing you but not with me. Sometimes
dreams slip poison, make

Me uncertain as to what is real, creating a dream-scape.

You make my brain shut up, I'd keep you

In whatever capacity you'd want me. What is real falls in a puddle

It's hard to say *I love you* when

The dream will not answer.

Dreamt tomorrow I become the other woman, laughingly

I do this to myself. and you were gone, like that.

and because tomorrow hasn't happened yet. I don't chalk this up
to a dream

I sit and whisper

It's hard to say *I want you.* When this isn't a dream.

Thing Called Mourning.

My mother calls me

Third time in a row on the

Fourth day of Shraddh to ask

If I fed her father yet. He's been dead

Over two decades now. The memory

Barely perseveres. We've learnt to mourn

The grief instead. I lie through my teeth

My hands run their hands on the

Dent of my head. I equate a lie to

An injury. I've been balancing my cosmic

Weight with my karmic balance. Recently

I fear I've become unmournable so

I tie my mouth up and plant tulips but

Halfway through I give up and throw

Soil in my mouth to spit back out

To turn to filth but I'm useful only

When I'm trying not to be so

Weed grows out of it. Life living outside

A still life.

My mother knocks on the phone

To ask me if I fed myself and I'm out of her

House so I lie without fear. I'm supposed to be fasting.

I remember a split second after I speak but

I don't cover up. The aperture in the room dims

And whatever sitcom I live in has an episode that

The viewers hate and everyone's breath abates.

Of course I moved out years ago but I will

Always be in my mother's house.

I cut the call off and feed the crows.

My mother calls me

Fourth time in a row-

Belly of the Beast

In the belly of the beast

You learn to dream. Ridges

Flutter like a breath and you almost impale

Yourself on its ribs and think of

How maybe god didn't make women from the ribs

Of a man but how, if you stay inside someone

Long enough, you pull something out to make it

Your own.

The streaming light that jumps in occasion doesn't

Hold your warmth so you tear out its tongue to

Keep you soft. You dream, however but not

Of ridges instead of how you learned to

Play für elise on illegible keys. How all things make the same

Sound till you hit them different.

Light has a shape, not curated by anything else

In your dreams, the sand around you is trying to accommodate
the shape

And you're next to your love

But your speech has been reduced to illegible infant noises

Mama for come here and don't leave and

Wah for water, feed me, it's not in me any longer.

In the belly of the beast, you do not dream of being in the belly of
the beast.

All dreams inside the belly of the beast occur inside the belly of
the beast.

When you wake up, you think of how

There are no elegies for the unmournable.

You do not consider your own mournability.

You walked into the belly of the beast, eyes wide open

The end of the tunnel. light blocked by a silhouette.

Poem As A Series Of Texts Sent Out When I Realised I Was In Love with you

My cat loves getting scratched with / A knife. A fake toy knife meant for / Plays and Movies and Pranks On Your Friends / one time someone switched it with a real knife / An honest mistake probably. / We had our routine. She played with it as she did. / That precarious thing in my hands/ She didn't get hurt but none of us realised until I nicked myself. / That's how I love him. I think. / Except I know the knife is real. / This is funny but talking to him / Makes my heart clench in a way / Where I understand why the /Comparison for the size of a heart / Is a fist. /This entire thing is disgusting. Feels like how / Cows eat food - mastication or wtv - like I have to / Down the entire thing at once. Accept it but it keeps / Coming back into my mouth - to be chewed like / A half digested desire rotting in my mouth. / Was listening to an NPR show on how more / Birds have / been dying for a variety of reasons / All over the world but a special kind, the kind / That hibernates south for the winter has been dying / Because it's sort of blind but temperature sensitive / Instead of flying south for winter it kept / Flying into people's thermostats. This is how / I feel about him. lol. Sort of blind but love sensitive and / Keep flying into his heart for a home / and realising that /I've flown into my death. / fuck the metaphors/ i want him./ npr show again on carrots becoming sweet to avoid death in the winter / how every time you bite into a sweet carrot/ it's the carrot saying i want to die / i set him up yesterday lmao. / i'm a carrot

No More Poetry - No Other Universe - Love Me In This One

After - "In another universe, we-"

No more of in other universes and cosmic findings and string theory and inventing dimensions to justify why you cannot like me. No more oranges and pomegranates and double texting theories. No more osmosis and parroting silence. No more physics and longing and star deaths. No more loving you like a dog and being betrayed like a man. No more not looking back. No more pretending like I wouldn't eat the apple if you asked, eat the heart if you asked. No more do to me what morning light does to dew by afternoon. No more forgive me in the morning, let me sin at night. No more desperation and you're tiny and heart hurts and breath cuts and heartbeat a hammer. No more manifestation reels. No more delulu is the solulu. No more of the heart is a wound afraid of admitting of being the wound and the sun, guileless and cruel. The sun, rotten motifs and borrowed identities and a silhouette of possibilities doing to the wound what the universe does to the existence of possibilities. no more, the Universe is an entrapment and the universe is a mother hoping and a father leaving and no more weariness. No more desperation. Come sit with me and hope for a minute. Breathe for a second. No more excuses, pool. Together some time and be tired with me for a second and let the border settle its wounds into the ground and

Let it heal for a second. No more apologies. No other universes.

No more metaphors. No more poetry. Touch me. Want me. Love

me in this one. Love me in this one. Love me in this- Love me in-

Love me- Love- L-

Anadya.

Let's run. Let's keep running. Swallow so much

Of a clear blue ocean that

Your reflection - mistakes you for - the empty sky

So much of this light is unbearable

The eclipse - hides only the dangerous part.

So little of this light can still kill.

I look for - clarity the morning - after an

Earthquake. To find - an answer or to find

Reason. I turn around and see

Your face and - the sun - no eclipse

Still unbearable - means so much

If I can see you under it.

I hear you - sing and think

If I had a siren song - it would be your voice.

You said - you'd see

My face if you ever saw Aphrodite.

I try to grab the ocean - and don't confess

If I ever had to find a God - It would be in your hug.

Let's run. Let's keep running. We've killed

All that is worth killing but if I had to save

All the things worth saving. I'd put my name on it

Only as an ode to you.

Anti Autism Diagnosis as A Love Letter

Doctor says the burden of proof lies with me to prove the non-autism within my brain so I whip out my journal - the one titled you & pull out a paper of diagnostic criteria. Doctor says persistent deficits in each criteria & I say you keep breaking the rules. Can't be persistent if it isn't true every time over & the doctor shakes his head & scribbles in a therapist journal. Doctor says highly restricted interests, an insular taste but. I watched Narcos for you & I watched Breaking bad for you & I watched the interviews & I watched the final of the match & I read about what cricket means, not my interests & I still hate them with a burning passion but follow them obsessively. These are yours. Doc says I exhibit hypo or hyper reactivity to touch & texture but. I hate sweat & you're a human radiator & I want to sleep inside your sweatshirt to remember that time on the roof where you were so close I could hear the hollow in your solar plexus your arrhythmia your mixed sweatshirt & who even wears a foul polyester cotton mix during winters but you & how I traced each texture top to bottom & how no hyporeactivity to your touch ever. I want to live in your skin, breathe your air & one night if we're close enough - to mistake your hand for mine & to kiss it. Doc says textbook case of severity in clauses. Doc says textbook case of sound avoidance

& echolalia but. Okay with sounds of heartbeat hollow of the heart & the gurgling of a stomach & your voice surrounded by nothing else & gravel down my throat & words formed in your lack of air & traced out shapes of sound and studying the disturbances in air around your mouth. Doc says deficits abound in my capacity for interpretation of social context but. You say five sentences a day and I have poems on each one of them. But. I know you're annoyed by my existence. but I know you're just being nice & where do we even go from me knowing. Doc says deficits in analysing own emotions - calls it alexithymia but. I know I love you. I know you don't. Doc rips a paper from his journal and calls it a diagnosis & says outliers don't get counted. I run my fingers over the loop of each word & say love isn't the outlier and doc nods and says. No. You are. I pause.

I Hope This Email Finds You

Greetings. I hope this email finds you

Not outside your dad's study or in ninth heaven.

I hope this email finds you before

You scab the tragedy out of your skin

Nubile, green stalks. Undone Grief.

I hope this email finds you on

The highway that no longer exists

Or before God does or before

The bout of existentialism does. I hope

This finds you living and thriving and (un)rotting

But traditionally.

I hope this email finds you before you open

Your mouth to talk to your dead mother but the

Words turn to birds and fly away and

Ablution isn't something attainable.

I hope the email finds you before

The kulfi melts melt before you get to the end and

The ends of your words don't curve inwards

And I hope the keffiyeh is unneeded for the frozen

And the clementine peels outward but doesn't drip

And you have someone to share it with and

Your grief isn't fragmented, milk pilling in the heat

And I hope the rot turns into something edible.

I hope this email finds you before the next

Tragedy does. I hope the email finds you

Outside the bathroom in the window creating

The world from scratch and screwing up and

Realising you're God and stretching skin on someone

Else and digging your mother's grave in your body.

I hope this email finds you before the next fall and

The next, this too shall pass.

I hope this email finds you in ways where you're still here

And don't intend to leave.

Breadth of Living

On mondays, I etch

The impossible breadth of loving

The tea plates will have our name on them

And the stories still, comprehend,

Flit with want. We could be real

I say. We could be loved. I say.

You nod and you walk away.

The days pass and it's still Monday

The next time you have it in you

To love me. Someone could love you

You Say, Another time, and I nod. You too.

I cook your favourite food and feed the

Empty table. Love grows- The dinner party tells us

I look over at you to laugh like

An inside joke festering but then I almost

Cry at the irony. I still. I sting. I cut the lemon and

End up chopping off my skin,

You think it's on purpose. I don't correct you.

On Tuesday, the first of its kind

The first of its time. I consider leaving you and

Then end up rolling on the floor with laughter.

Love festers like mould on the wall.

This house is inorganic and I refuse to leave her.

The bus is not still but you are so I lurch into you,

Often. Buildings pass the years in the window. Trees

Undressed, skinny bus pole jaywalking into existence.

I pulled this love from the scrapyard from

Some planet that does not exist anymore

And I think of your theory that the only thing that

Has enough want to kill is love and I think of the

Planet, burning and I start to love my skin.

I exist only in relation to you or

The cat you kept for summer before you

Decided that abandoning only counts if you

Didn't give birth to the thing.

On Wednesday, the last and only of its kind.

I look up at the sky in July where

The rain is like cracked egg on the sun

Mewling like a stadium in the wind.

I swell open and the sound crackles before it

Becomes itself and you come home

To leave me and I nod.

This planet lived because you could not love me.

I pulled this body from a scrapyard

With no blues to dress it up.

I cry for a day and scramble an egg

To create the sky and say

I will grow yet.

One Act Play Where We-

Mom coughs as she enters a dusty doorstep, she waves her hand to clear the air like dust is something tangible and not just proof of inexistence. Nothing happens. <u>Mom</u> is glistening with what appears to be water but her hair is dry. Mom is backlit and she looks oddly ominous like a biblically accurate angel with the correct amount of eyes.

Mom: This could be home too. We could live here.

I shakes their head. I starts taking each limb off periodically and putting it on the dining table. Mom helps pull off the last hand with a harsh tug and almost falls back. The stage blacks out and the table is now a feast with the limbs in the middle.

Chatter can be heard distantly, people sound like they are approaching.

I: They're going to eat me alive here *waves head over the table due to the lack of limbs*

Mom snorts suddenly. She grabs I's hand and takes a bite but her face scrunches with disgust.

Mom: They've undercooked you here too. Nothing's ever right. Goldilock had it easier.

I: They're going to eat me alive here.

Mom continues eating the hand, her face relaxing gradually.

I: I'm scared

Mom stops. She Appears to be having a realisation, her face turns comical.

Mom: I'm scared

I: Yes. Maybe we should go back home.

Mom: Back home.

I: We haven't found an answer yet.

Mom: Answer yet.

Mom appears to be in a trance

I: I think I'm going to be scared forever.

Mom: Forever.

I: We'll never find a home. Will you be here?

Mom: Here.

Mom resumes eating I's hand

I sighs then sloppily puts their face down and starts eating their leg, pulling at the ligaments. White fluid flows out.

I: Scared?

Mom: Scared.

I: Okay. Together then?

Mom: Together.

People start entering and taking a seat. They start eating. The curtain closes.

Minting

As a child, minted in some inherent way

I wanted to be God so I could be heard.

So powerful, a voice across millennials and oceans

And though the world was then,

Only, this borough to the next.

I was learning to comprehend it could be bigger

Because whoever he was, had to come from outside of it.

Ironic to think that God didn't make me religious, the Devil did.

Turned me devout and flailing and praying

Every morning and every day.

If you're there. Save me; Save me; Save me.

Never an answered prayer from the sinner

Because that's just punishment.

Never being saved as the disbeliever so I trained it

Out of my vocabulary. I started with. God it's getting hard again.

Save me. I'm okay with

Dying twice before I stop believing in you.

Then eventually. No more prayers and no more words.

I'd sit silently on his lap and think of who is watching

Then call him a voyeur for watching before no longer existing.

I lied. I had to die thrice before I stopped believing in him.

God had to be a man to not give two shits about what he created.

But okay, you know this story. The pipeline of disbeliever to
believer to dis-

I have nothing new to give but you're still listening.

So let's train this into your vocabulary. You can survive dying but

You never come out of living unscathed. Love is a tangled mess
inside a car crash

Turned inwards then upwards then the safety belt is tangled in
your heart

And it kills you. That's love. That's what you didn't give God and
God killed you

Okay then. Learn to love in ways that aren't brutal then. Train this
into your vocabulary

Let the thought into your brain turn before it sours.

Love is to be saved and mostly, time saves you.

You can learn to love to live because loving is time.

If no one's looking. I get to love temporally instead.
Disbeliever and sinner and unanswered and praying.

I get to love. The end is a window to the beginning.

God Outside First Grade

Memory is fluid. Persimmons

Look for answers. We try to shift to

Where we are still loved so we lie. I lie.

Only of how I missed home so much

That the mutilation of prayer settled

The fingerprint of the sun embezzling

Deep within my skin, a cancer but

Mostly proof. We lived here where there

Was a place. Remember how before

We gave up god as rebellion we'd

Sing about Mary and her sheep.

For so long that Mary was reunited

Somewhere off in the world. A landscape

Coloured itself and a man uncorked his

Flask and suddenly the flaming wasteland

Is bearable again. Set the task to flaming for

The sins that led up to this. God in my

Sandwich. God in my juice. God in the

Mountain, judging. Most mornings I wake

To try to return to a state of belief that nursery

Rhymes let me get away with. Jack on the

Hill. Surviving. Jack with the sugar. Lying.

Loved. Humpty Dumpty. Mutilated. Found.

The rhetoric has a place only

Until someone proves the answer. How much

Can we get away with. A thousand years

Simmer with grief. A pot where the flame

Is always too low. It's your imperative, your faith

But we touch the wielded blood

Separated by a hundred empires. The promise

Grossly misrepresented. Spit on a wall like

A Too good paan1 that outlived itself.

All of the lake blanket nights where I

Floated a dead man's float then walked

Out and my body grossly hyper aware of

Itself. Thud. Beat. Flicker. Answer.

My body like a bloated goldfish that

Hadn't been replaced yet. I strut back home

To a place where I can live. The mountain greens

The flame is finally dying out.

Notes on A Pre-Killing Myself Era

I

Days crack again. Mint dew cascades.

Winter pretending to be summer pretending to be spring.

I learnt to be warm on a random day in July.

The summer when everything died

And they told us Autumns are sometimes indecisive

Same year I learnt that ethylene is conversive.

That you can die because everyone else is dying.

I tried to kill myself because my brother died

But that comes later.

I always want to live first. Okay Then. That's where the story
starts.

II

God is sitting on the window sill behind the barracks.

God is soaking wet. God has rain in the winter

God said it can't snow this close to the equator.

Each drop flops its way from his hair to

Transform mid fall to fly off. I say I want to live

So I try to catch the water to drink it but I'm bad at

Catching so I end up eating dirt which was

Also flying and was more so God looks at me

With disgust and says. This is why you couldn't be a person.

I don't get sad. Autumn trees twirl around itself

The soil gulps itself down and I think of what it's like

To be dirt with purpose and think I've discovered what it means to
be human.

God shakes his head in the way that means No. Stop.

But I'm from a different country so I think he's saying yes.

I wonder what's universal and then feel the existential dread

Of finding God looking through my window.

And get my answer.

III

Is this where death starts? No. Wait.

The colours chafe here which isn't to say

That they fade but they die.

Bright red roses fall. Leaves, still green.

You can die before learning to die.

God, sits in Kirtan Trees, no longer overlooking

I fail to be bastardised if I cannot be seen so I start to sin.

I want to live, yet. My body still greening from asbestos.

I start eating dead things but I don't kill them

Which I think absolves me but it doesn't but not

In the way you'd think. I don't have their death

On my hands. I just have my living on mine but okay.

That comes later. I pull apart leaves that died

While they were alive because they are green then

Don't mourn their deaths but mourn instead the lack of crunch

I kiss and I clean and I flutter from man to woman

This isn't the sin. The sin starts

When I think I'm a person. So I start trying.

I become a good person in July which means that

I smile and break walnut seeds by hand to feed

Him but he's fraying like mangrove trees pruning out

Of water so I go to God to be seen and ask for water

But he realises I have sinned so he looks away.

I scoop water falling from him and this time

It doesn't fly away. I throw it against him.

He keeps fraying. I get sad.

When autumn comes around

There is nothing left for autumn to take

So it comes and passes and doesn't grieve its purpose

I am greener still but I've learnt

That you can die if everyone is dead.

So, I stop.

IV

Is there where the dying starts?

No. This is where it ends. It gets boring.

Days crack indubitably. Mint julep humidifies

On large glasses outside hotels mother goes

To revive the living.

I get told that pretending makes you a person

So I try it out but this time.
God isn't around and I'm sneaking into

Rituals so I explore.

The roses die after rotting so

I bleed to keep them red

In company, I seek the end

But ethylene crawls its way into existence to

Reverse something in me.

Something crawls its way into my mouth

And I become dirt with purpose and think.

Oh. Okay.

I will succumb to the living &

I will come out of it scathed.

letter to my brother on a tuesday morning where i stop mourning

His departure left

A long radiation shadow that

Persisted beyond his survival

When my brother died

I rushed to his room to

Tell him about his death and

Spoke to the empty room

About death being a metaphor

For a tilting the world and

I wondered if ghosts could get

Claustrophobic. Then the tin

We kept him in started shaking

Every rainstorm and I had my

Answer from beyond the grave

Even dead he knew more than I did

Even dead, he wanted me to know more.

You did your laundry the day

Before you killed yourself which meant

A lot of things but mostly that nothing smelled

Like you and the night before. You

Put your skull wings necklace on my throat

And looped it twice till my carotid twinged

Often I thought of how you could have killed me

But recently I think about how your name doesn't make me

Want to throw up anymore.

You died a few times before I believed it.

The first when you swallowed rat poison and

A time of death was declared and somewhere

Off in the world, a glass shattered for

bad luck and some for good.

You were a cold body at your wake,

Clinging to sleep and we all performed in a haze

I wrote a requiem and bought an ouija board.

The second your memory shattered somewhere

In my brain and I stopped grieving you.

When I try to remember your face, I see an

Outline of your smile turned in on itself and sweat

Sticking to the basketball and your jersey

You used to say elegy are just words

That can't contain you so I wrote you this.

The third when I broke a glass for good luck

And bad and grazed it across my neck

Looped with your pendant. There's only

A tallness to death that feels unbreachable

Until you see the sky so I started climbing walls.

The last when I opened your diary, dust embedded

Like a ghost coming to life and I read of your love

And started mourning you.

the car ride to the hospital after the third time i try to kill myself

Asked myself to stay or go but

Fifteen missed calls over one missed text. So I stay.

I have nothing to give but the things I can define

And the things I can't.

The traffic tilts to form a thinning wall—On the way to the hospital

I can't stop giggling. The moon is full and motile. In a reflection, I can see me

In a reflection, everything is dark and the blood resembles only itself.

A metaphor's likeness drips through the cracks.

I sluice a fruit and liken it to my wrist. The peels fall on the road

Framing two houses. You could put every building in this city

On a map and still be left with white space.

Mom stills. She has learned to fester like a wound. Visible and inflamed.

The moon glowers like an injury.

Worst part about being hurt is being reminded I'm mortal.

Living is an exercise in irony.

Dad shakes & points out the balloon seller. He

Asks me if I want a heart. I dig

My hands deeper into my wrists

Something squelches with it and the

Blood likened to blood floats like the moon

Flits into existence between corporates.

Today, I will fathom the impossible distance from here to there.

Yesterday, I thought I could make it.

The body is a plant turned in on itself. After

The third attempt, I suspect I secretly want to live

The moon giggles. Then me. Then my mother.

The traffic gives out and the Earth turns in on itself

To bring back the day. I catch some blood and think.

I can learn & then I will know something about having a body.

Elegy For Unbecoming

In my dream, I'm still correct so

you still love me. The desperate

Roads singed with loneliness. I

Am sitting in the night stool that

You promised to make when we

Have a home and I file that note

For the future. The one where I'm

Drunk and we're both some place safe.

This time I try to quiet the cicadas so I

Can make out what you're trying to

Say and I hope you say that you don't

Want to leave either. The ghosts always

Haunt but we have those frozen orange

Bars that taste awful. You look at me

Four times removed. Your eyes. Your glasses.

My glasses. The painting you thought

I lived in. We are all trying to make

It and be worthy of making it. So we

Chase the bad men and hope it balances

Out whatever cosmic balance we've tipped

Over by loving each other.

Instead we take the metro and you tell

Me stories but every story begins

Drunk with you and ends the same

Way. You make me worried. You

Make me confuse my hope for

Prayer. What can I love? Is it

Of this Earth. Sometimes when the

Light corners you. You look like a

Poisoned apple at the end of a story

And you look like you could love me

I am loved by what's of this Earth

The dream buffers. What happens

Next is always incomprehensible.

The too white hospital bed and

How the mausoleum was before the ICU

Which should have been a warning but I

Read out Nirmal Verma to you and hoped

For the best. Maybe the tragedy cancels

Out. If enough people grieve in the story

I don't have to grieve for you. Remember

We took those scissors and said we'd

Have an exhibition of stolen things from

The time you almost died and that's a

Funny story to tell at the dinner table before

Asking questions like. Do you think I was

Supposed to be dead. How we stitch the

Torn upholstery because we all want to be

Worth it to someone. Sorry I'm a broken

Thing. You love me anyway. The desperate

Roads lined with yarrows. Still blooming and

I look over at you. You're not a ghost. I keep

Sleeping. I don't mourn you.

Elegy for the Unbecoming 2

For the longest time

I sat in your chair

To see the impr-

ession when I left

Proving that you're

Still here. I turned

Off the light to

Pretend that the

Light shivering of

Winter trees were

Your footsteps coming

Home. That they meant

something more than how

the Earth turns on itself

To keep you warm

And cold and grieving

but nothing means more

because the world turns

in on itself. Another

Winter. Another summer

Another rain and You're

still not here which

means that things

are constant. Outside,

the stars Disassemble

Into individuals when we

Aren't looking and Trying

to turn them into art.

This is the best day

Since 1874 when

I was still alive but

It didn't matter so

I turn the tv on, Madonna

Plays but the news doesn't

So we are happy; inside

The plant tries to grow in the

Pot and hopes that roots are

Enough to keep hold and

To live despite, inspite.

Someone is listening.

The ad says on TV so I

Say 'I love you'

To test it out and hope

For a response.

Maybe the lack of it

Is the answer but I

Shake my head and think.

How stupid. How insane.

And think about how your impr-

ession would laugh at that

So I get up from the sofa and

Smile at the dip in space

The Girl talks about Symbols of Oppression and Eats out of the Trash

I wanted to be more

Than the symbols of my oppression so

I refused to get married. We are susceptible to

Trash and filth. To return to what may be

The rat survives the night but the fish

laughs at it for it. I don't have it in

Me to kill. The sunlight pillages through

The dustbin because we are all hungry

For something that only the waste can give

Then the skunk scours the trash and

Finds some abdicated joy that he can

Steal and suddenly he's happier than all

Of us. I try to take umbrage at questions

About my appearance but then the other shoe

Falls and I realise I can walk out of here.

Maya the milkman. Maya the miser

Maya the next door neighbour and I

Try to remember their names but I just

Call them. Sweetheart, how's your day been

This is a good time to be alive. You will find

A jaunty face and not think about how close

It sounds to gaunt. Mollified. A text from an old

Friend and I have to be honest. I thought she was

Dead but the leviathan text asks "what was that movie"

And we know what the movie is because love's labour lost

The movie. Girl at the barn. Wild western in Asia. Kitsch and
tacky

Awful actors and I try to scour through my trash

That hasn't been cleared out in years and find

The Leviathan movie for the Leviathan text and

This is a nod to what language can't steal from us.

The same memory though coloured sepia by years lost and I

Think of how long she waited to text me. The racoon

Tries to hand me something and it's a poster.

Bad movie from years ago. I text her back

Learning To Drive

A millennia of being loved

Passes through the windows.

In paths, I never see speed breakers

The man says I will die because I went too quick one day.

I liken myself to Icarus and call it a fall of pride.

Suddenly

Everything stills, then halts

and some homage is paid to the truck passing us by.

After a millennia of free will,

the answer to natural order still evades me.

I pulled this body out of the water for many reasons

But mostly so I could be loved.
Somewhere, an orbit misaligns and something

Agrees and almost makes sense.

I brush the speed off the bike then flit

I am alive but only as something that can be perceived secondarily.

In relation to fissured bones and a smile.

Sometimes, loving becomes so big

I can almost see it in colours and have it swallow us whole.

I fall on gravel and I splatter like paint or brain from the twelfth
floor.

I second my skin to something hard. Then rough.

Then something almost real. I move and speed and halt.

For a spring. I am here. When this is over

I will go home and be a stillborn again.

Go Fish

Father says to us

Let's go fish. If the bait has their fins

Caught on a hook

You have to kill it

If it bleeds anywhere else.

You have to let it go.

I belch and try to forgive him

The tragedy of a choice is the lack of it

Of course we have to feed ourselves

Death has never been an option.

The untamed monster of my grief

Writhes and begs.
We all huddle in the car to kill

Whatever soft part is still left in us

Most of my body is soft scar tissue

Here. Can you smell it?

The smell of a dead thing crawling up

The floors as proof. The last soft thing

In you is dead. He killed it. It's rotting.

We nod and take out our bait and hooks

A fish's fin catches on the hook and I try

To cry and ask to be forgiven.

The tattooed priest in black is on the other boat

I look at him in tears and he asks me to kill it

I take the fish back to the aquarium to let it heal

I wanted to be good. Wanted to go to the house of god.

The fish looks at me accusingly from the fish bowl.

What's food from the start gets eaten.

The fact is not a tragedy. The grief is.

Heaven-bid and Unmournable.

The Paracetamol sets in as Mia

Sings next to me. There's a dead

Cow on the road. Not a tragedy

By any means. Not a cow hit by a

Car. Not a life trying to live.

Only a cow sleeping

Middle of the farm. Lavender tomb

Which is to ask. How sad am I allowed

To be. The dead cow tries to

Get up and fight me into being scared

I'm scared of all the cows until.

I'm a chocolate fountain trying.

Heavenly bliss. Christ is in my sandwich

Which doesn't feel far off

From consuming his flesh which doesn't

Feel on brand for the whole concept of sinning

How much can I get away with before

The cocoa sheds its skin to reveal that it's wheat

And I'm a dead cow in a beautiful tomb

Heaven-bid and unmournable.

Untitled

The Wind is furious. Your t-shirt ripples against your body.

(A silhouette that can't decide.)

You perched on my windowsill giggling. Ten stories up.

I stand halfway across so I can catch you.

Tell us about the time I asked

Do you ever mourn and

You palmed at my dresser and asked me why

I don't wash the grief off of those thing but then you pulled out an
unmarked jungle graveyard out of your bag and your eyes
twinkled as you threw it over at me.

You, sanctimonious bastard. You, widow out of mourning. You,
bird in migration finding a home. You, wedding on the knees
saying yes.

Tell us the story where it's winter again and we are

Digging up the graveyard to eat the bodies for warmth and no one

Has any humanness left on their bones.

You, percolating in the middle of the story. You, twittering as you stumble and steady yourself. Me already on the ground of the building hoping to break your fall.

Me, speckled blood on linoleum. Me, filthy mop scrubbing it out. Me, grief stricken widow still in mourning.

The bodies in the graveyard are full of soil which is to say they are still full and you ask me

How much do you think death can still touch us? How much does it want to?

I'm covered in my own blood and I have those wolverine gloves which means that I like tearing the flesh off things.Forget the blood. Forget what made us like this which is that we are all sick and inhuman and we tried to be canaries when we were mourning but

We went on that jungle safari and we walked on the rope but you fell and those grass stains touched you ugly and dry like the snake on the 99th box when we played snakes and ladders.

The wind dies to give you form. The rippling stops and so you are nothing.

Me, knife scalding my body to become like yours. Me, dagger filled clawed vultures at the end of the world crying in satin. Me, nameless formless looking for an unmarked grave.

And then there's you perching over my body making it yours. You, mausoleum at the beginning of a hospital. You, glimmer of being. You, widow out of mourning.

I'm still alive after a long fall. Which means that I get to confess.

I become Raven Talkative which means that I don't have anything original to say but I'm saying everything anyway. Which means that at the end of the world we all want to be loved in desperate gruesome ways. Which means that I get to confess that I wish someone would love me enough to die for me or kill for me or whatever the poets tell you should happen in love. Which means that I learn enough from people that When I go to the fair and get on the ferris wheel, my eyes don't bleed anymore and the gravity calls out to us like My god. Look at how stupid they are. And I nod and smile and bow. I'm so wrong in that I'm so right but I'm human again so it doesn't matter. And then there's that thing again. The loop never ends.

The wind is furious. Your t-shirt ripp-

cathood

Did you know that the oldest domesticated cat is almost 10,000 years old.

The only proof we have of that is that they were buried with their human bones

Purposefully. That's a thing in archaeology.

Shown Purpose.

Of course we had the entire sky to embrace

Of course we chose our cats.

We learned to love before we knew we could die

My cat steps on my keyboard and I only think

Of how I'd like to be buried with her.

Winter Night Sadness

Look. Winter rested

Over your shoulder

And we sat next to the fire

The warmth engulfed us like

Love letters between two gods

Kept over a millenia. Collecting dust

But being slid out of their hiding spot

To be seen.

We are all meant to be loved.

Gnocchi

Octopuses have three hearts, a

Sanguin collaboration of liminal

Spaces. They need all that to live

And nine brains to understand what

I know. An octopus has three hearts to

Understand. That is how I love you.

You, frazzled pink shirt, the only one

Doing work, clearing a table unwieldy

For me to sit on. I remember that you

Shook my hand and I wanted it to be

held for the rest of my time on this

Poor peasant Earth. I thought I wanted

To know how to be loved but what was

Between us didn't need nine brains.

You said you wanted to make me

Gnocchi and then you went back to

Work. I knew I was loved. As some

unloved things are meant to be loved.

Anatomy Of A Long Dead Royal Family

Each morning my lineage burns itself

I keep ashes of the effigy

My great grandma had the kind

Of money that comes with castles

Built with escapeways

The kind where you have a garden to hunt for sport

She learnt to shoot to avenge her husband's death

Ashes. I wish I had the courage to love what wasn't there

Each morning. I trace back the events

That led up to this. I try to figure out

What parts of me aren't stolen.

I am pink. I can look green in certain lighting. I've always lived in
the castle. I don't know how to hold a gun. I swallow flowers in
hopes of turning into a garden. I dine with skunks and ask to be

forgiven.

My grandmother had the motility

Of a colour blind colour wheel.

Her garden had peacocks that crooned. She knew of caution

Her daughter learned to throw it to the wind.

My mother learned to keep a bird cage and to not

Abandon the things she loves.

She went fishing and only killed the fishes

With broken fins. I wish I had the courage to

Let things out of their misery.

Some nights, I think I have the courage to save the world

Most mornings I wake up and I continue living.

The lilies are opening up.

There's still enough left in this world

To be loved by it.

I carve out my lineage. I get to continue it yet.

Valentine: A list of texts that make me and break me.

"I am well liked by the world again" "You always were. The world just hid it."// "You called me back? I didn't get a notif" "I think so. It was pouring. The clouds cried and the oceans raged. It was for our love"// *flying over the pacific, buying expensive data to send me an i love you text* "Now the pacific knows of my love for you. It's never going away."// "I don't need you to be an easier person to love. Loving you is instinct at this point. That's all I need and I never want it to stop"// "me: you love religiously, it's one of my favourite things" ''them: I hadn't known religion till I'd been with you"// "It's you. It's always been you."// "I will always choose you. If I am without memory, my love will guide me to you"// "You mean so much to me in ways you couldn't imagine. I think of you when I listen to Everglow by Coldplay and when I think of what makes me want to be a better person" // "hey hey hey. What's up? All good? You okay?"// "Everyone begins and ends their reference points with themselves but you, you're the transcendent continuum. You exist across all timelines" // "and the birds will forgive us and the oceans will forgive us and they will be unrelenting but they will be there"// "you have a very real and scarily big capacity for love and it's going to take me a good minute to wrap my mind around it BUT. BUT. What you have going for you is that I don't feel like you're just throwing it at me. You know me. You've been around. We didn't just meet. This is like our third lifetime together what the fuck I love you"// "Insane isn't it. I would fold up the ocean and deliver it if you asked me. "Love you back" is an oversimplification"//

Sopping Aspirations

All my dreams are wet. They mean aspirations. Dreams always mean aspirations but I've never had those so I pretend. The subjectivity of the throne poured down our threats. We need to be our weight's worth in gold and our measuring tapes are skewed. It's against our favours but okay. I count back and try to hold. I've always wanted to modulate the mirror to sound different so I could finally have a friend. My axons are firing slowly to the next one so the message reaches late. My sister says my bone broke last month and I've been walking on it since. Right. The pain is finally reaching . Twenty days till the world ends and I'm not ready. I have four dents on my head from growing up with a crown too small which surprisingly isn't a metaphor. *knocks on my head* Are we going to get out of here? Sweat drips and it almost looks like a waterfall. Flick. Flick. Flick. The table looks up at me annoyed like it's my fault, I'm just alive. What do you want me to do here? Hello? Look, let's go into the forest and I'll show you the mess no one is willing to own and maybe you'll feel better about being loveless. The headset digs into my skin like it's trying to find a home(no one wants to be abandoned) There's an old abandoned wood-house we can go to cool down which sounds important but it just means I can scrape at something and make an impression. Proof of life. Maybe we will eat the magnolias on our way back and let flowers grow in our stomach on the way back and finally you'll be beautiful. The question is I have a lot of paper but it doesn't seem to serve a purpose so I go to a tarot reader. What's the answer? "Did you stuff yourself with daffodils and cherries" Yes but that doesn't mean anything. You're trying to be a garden girl but you're a person. Your girlhood is beyond its ability to prove itself. It transcends molecular space and physics turns its back shyly. The dendrites and the axons separate and go to sleep. The world is ending and the pain turns sour like spoiled milk on a hungry day. My earphones tangle and I cry and ask is this what terror tastes like and she takes it and untangles it for me. I nod. Look. Here. That was my angel. I met mine and it was gorgeous. Every mess I make, I grow more entombed within her and I said. Look. There's the aspiration they were talking about. I want to be her. La. La. La. She sings over me. I nod and go to sleep.

Elegy for Slasher films and Self Portrait as the First Girl.

The last time I was in a room like this was when I dreamt I was the first girl in a slasher film. I am not the same girl I was three years ago which is to say - I'm barely a girl anymore. Am I allowed to grow up? I've been living, touching the world hesitantly like I'm licking the lips of someone I love and not licking my own lips when they get cracked as year old concrete roads with weed growing out of them in winter which is to say, I try to elaborate everything as metaphors so you forget what I was trying to say because I never know what I'm trying to say. Anyway. Slasher movies. Of course I watch slasher movies with popcorn and a brain that refuses to be afraid of jump scares. I'm afraid of walking home alone at night, not bad cinematography. Slasher movies. That is to say that I know what angst means especially when it can be put down on paper. Angst is an origami man holding hands with another origami man holding hands- until they meet up in a long enough chain that they cover the top of the board and now there's unity in this world but it's made out of paper. My mom says I did the teen angst thing at ten which is to say I understood the complexity of ridicule before all of you. Which is to say I understood how things worked and how much I hated being the first girl in a slasher film before any of you. Which is to say. I became the first girl in a slasher film because I was the first one to realise what narrative I was stuck in. The first damnation is simply knowing. You cannot walk into the deep, desperate hell without first knowing the door to it. Anyway. My individuality complex damned me. Whatever. My therapist says I have a raging individuality complex. She's so wrong, I'm just the most unique person in all of existence. I'm the only one of me. Anyway. The first time I was in a room like this was the last time I watched a slasher film because I was scared I was going to be casted in one real time soon enough but I'm weaving metaphors through things like embroidery patches that cover every part of my bare skin. Anyway. You get this. You get it. I don't watch slasher films anymore. Anyway. That doesn't stop me from being damned.

Where Dead Birds Go To Die

Dead bird on the rooftop/It takes me a while till I recognise what fossils mean/ Skeletal Wings, that is to say/ We caught a dead thing and then we killed it anyway/ We saw how beautiful the dead thing is and we decided to keep it that way/ Nothing beautiful stays beautiful unless it's dead/ At its best/ We killed it and doused it in apricot milkshake and the backyard after rain/ We killed it to make it beautiful and then we kept it in a book/ A dead bird is a dead bird till it's a bookmark/ We could never have been happy with just a feather. We've wanted from the start/We've consumed from the start/Want/That is to say/We caused the apocalypse. The first emotion to cascade the apocalypse down the dominoes as they fall but there's no order. We've been arranging dominoes along a line and we haven't come back to the start yet. The world is a circle until you can't make it back home. The apocalypse. That is to say. The first time I saw a dead bird. I wanted to be nothing else. I've always wanted to die beautiful. Oh look at you, you poor sweet thing. So young. So much potential. Taken too soon. I will ruin myself beyond comprehension but I will be left without scarring. Oh you beautiful thing, what you could have been. Fine. Okay. Tired metaphor. Dead bird in a cage but the cage is made of dead remains. Skeletal Leaves. We are bound by the very thing that created us. Look at me sweetheart. We are going nowhere. Okay. Fine. Nothing better to keep it in.

Bones are the oldest weapons. That is to say. A beautiful thing is a beautiful thing when it's dead. An ugly thing is an ugly thing especially when it's dead. That is to say. You still have use beyond preservation. You can be the things that wars are fought with. I can be the things that wars are fought over. Fine. Every place for a dead bird is a dead place. Haunted architecture. Rooms that never end. Doors that never begin. A house stopped from being a house. Okay. Fine. We are a thousand years young and a hundred days old. Every narrative is an old one. No one has a new story. No one will ever have a new story. We've lived through this, now what? The audience always knows. The room is full of people who know everything we don't but they can't tell us anything. You and I die at the end of this. We will always be dead birds at the end of the play. The audience will always know. It ends with me bleeding out in your arms. The vulgarity of bleeding out in front of you. Obscene. We can be intimate all we want. But you've always been inside me and now I will always be outside you. Try scrubbing me out of your hands. I want to bleed out in a doctor's hands. The vulgarity of bleeding out in love is obscene. I want to die in a room with no parts of us. I've never wanted to die at home. A blank room. A stranger. A scalpel. A chance of survival but we all know how this ends. I was never going to make it out of this alive. That's been the entire point. The lord's fruits are poisonous. New life always comes from death. It's spittle. It's a spitoon. We've been doomed from the start. Pathetic. A bird is a dead bird when it goes to a place without a tomb. All people are lovable. But we will never die as sweetly as turtles do. Birds will always die homelessly. We should start carrying our own tombs. The audience will throw their clothes at me when I die and you will still clutch me and you will sob and the people will sob and everyone will cry and I will be full of blood. Beauty cannot be embraced with roses, They needed me to feel what has been felt. They've known from the start. They want me to feel the knowing. They've known from the start and that is their tragedy but this. This is ours. All tragedies are good tragedies if they start with a dead bird and end with one. The birds are different in that they are the same. The only good bird is a dead bird. All dead birds are the same birds. It's a good tragedy when the skeletal wings fossilise and a child picks up the imprints of beauty on an eroded rock in sand and takes it back home because everything beautiful stays beautiful as long as it dies young.

Anagha.

["Insane isn't it. I would fold up the ocean and deliver it if you asked me. "Love you back" is an oversimplification]

There are a million ponds for a million oceans for a million ways to dance it spins me downside up what starts at the foot to how i see this world nothing leaves me bereft of astonishment but you make me more wondrous than most. You say you'd take the things i say and put them on a tote bag to explain to the world that i exist a million oceans on a million planets all are so big to mean something so simple if i had to pick what was divine there'd be the words iso and your hands on it. A million ships on a million oceans and millions more with no anchor and what does this all mean if not the answer to why we're here and that is a type of hummingbird still which means a lot but mostly that i want to sit in the flask on the burner and stay for a minute and watch my molecules separate. Language is an attempt at memory which explains what im doing here but not what the rest of it means which is that you are an ocean cradling movement you are soundless grief you're trying to reach a shore that you're busy keeping the dead things alive thinking you have a hollow where there is none what i mean is there are a million ponds for a million oceans for a millions ways to dance and my molecules are separating with you as witness or my molecules are separating because it's you witnessing and you afraid of the shore still

swimming is waiting at the other end i love you as an attempt at
meaning you say you love me back which is an oversimplification
but really we're a glamorous hell and i love the world as an imprint
of you and the way sand didn't first exist as sand but as everything
else and now it will be nothing else.

Complicity

Aaron Bushnell is dead -

No longer complicit in genocide -

My chronically online Gen Alpha class asks me about him

And I have to go take a walk.

The wind is warm in February. I think

Of what the weather becomes like after 50 bombs

Dropped in a day. I teach the concept of heat in class.

They're learning to count. Every child in Gaza who

Hasn't learnt to count yet but is now a statistic.

I'm teaching them phonetics with the names of the dead.

Jamal. Rahman. Salem. Fatima. Fayena. Ibrahim.

I listen to the ordnance raincloud scream in a video.

Mia asks me what to do when someone is screaming for help.

I don't tell her to point a gun at them.

These are not equal sides. Occupier and Occupied.

I bring a box to class to show how large Gaza is.

I teach them "Occupation" before I teach them hope

And cats and strong and girl and boy.

I hold their faces when they do not cry and

Hope they understand. I hold their faces and think

Of how I would kill for them and I think of how the war

Has been alive for longer than they have. Complicit.

Their faces, curious and beckoning. Their faces, hopeful.

Their faces, alive. I try to change the curriculum and get fired on

My third day. I take a walk.

I grab an adult and shake them and ask.

Did you know that there's a genocide? There's a genocide
happening here.

Would you burn yourself? Do you wonder what you would do?

Are you listening? Do you care?

My chronically online Gen Alpha goes home and teaches

Their parent what it means to self immolate.

Somewhere, off in the world. Another child becomes a number

Before learning what the number means or before sounding

Out the words to their name but my kids, alive and kicking.

Are learning to kick in this world. I continue walking. I teach them

Genocide before I teach them Mine or Yours.

Are you complicit? Are you learning what it means?

After Colorado Springs - I measure the buoyancy of my own existence

I'm floating in a way where I'm still alive.

I go out dancing and I fit into people

Like two dimensional shapes fit onto paper.

What's home but the first place that agrees to let you be?

I'm floating again in the first place

That told me

That a monster is not such a bad thing to be.

A hand flits like a bird. Too fast to prove that I'm too slow

A voice above asks me to duck. I try to question if it's god's voice

How desperate the gazes turn.

When monsters turn to love other monsters.

We duck and I'm floating in a way where they

Are trying to kill me.

What's left when the place that agreed to let you be?

Isn't let be? Wasn't I supposed to be the monster?

I'm haunted by

The proof of how illegitimate I am. A monster isn't supposed to
float.

We float still.

I go out dancing and I fit into people.

I twist into enough shapes that I can duck all the bullets.

spotify wrapped comes out as danny masterson's jury fails to reach verdict

You spent 545,686 minutes this year being a silly goose!

That's the fifth story in a row

I've started itching away at old scars, soon enough

They'll be new wounds again.

I've always been one for karmic justice, as above and so below, what goes around, comes around and I'm trying. To believe that still.

What's another man getting away with something

If no one knows he got away with it.

Your Spotify Wrapped says your top artist is Taylor Swift and that you're a devoted listener but you start your mornings as a hopeless romantic and end your days cycling your way back to some place where you can be angry. Your attention span is fifteen seconds and your ability to hold someone accountable is shorter still.

One lucky artist was your number 1

I'm seething with rage and all the

Unnamed women that had to be named for this trial

Are listening to their spotify wrapped as they never get a job again.

Names are all associated with things but this one means

"Our employer thinks you'd be a liability to hire. We wish you
good luck for your future!"

Your audio aurora was Wistful and Lovesick

I open Twitter so I can tweet at the victims

I know how little words mean especially when it's about bravery

"You're so brave" I wish that could buy you food "Hope you're
doing well" I know you aren't

"Karma is rea-"(l for everyone but a white man with a following)

I end up retweeting my moot's top five songs of the year instead.

Under the Plantation of a tree, Dead Nutrients,

Weed tastes

Like the time my father drowned me

When trying to teach me how to have fun.

As distant as my father.

Weed makes me as far away

From myself

As my father.

I was the original sin.

I committed the original blasphemy

I stood on a horizon and said

This body was not for me.

I have been blasphemous longer than I've been alive

Because then I chose to love all wrong too.

The first woman I loved was

Sour, like she was

Pickled in vinegar.

Like her existence only made sense in something else.

She was so incomplete, she made me sob.

The next man I ended up loving.

Was so full, so complete. There was no space for me.

But I have been loved.

I have been loved

Like the new stalks on a plant

Tender. Nubile. Naive. Soft.

I've been loved so softly. Even when there wasn't space for love.

Questions outside Interrogation Rooms

Q: Did you kill them?

Silence.

Okay. Fine. You knew they were dead because you wanted to kill them but you didn't. Intent is a throwaway nest. No bird wants someone else. There is no home if the weight of building it didn't crush you under itself. You will build a home where the ropes that hold it up are hung from the sky.

Q: Do you know how they died?

Silence.

Okay. Fine. You know how they died. You also know how God died. God died when we were five with a dead dad. God died when there was a fish, there is a fish in the aquarium as you walk out,

and it looks like them. Dead fish. Matching spots.

Q: Do you care how they died?

Silence.

Okay. Fine. Dead people are worth more than dead fishes. To be fair you didn't kill either. Dead things have a way of resembling each other. Different you come, rot you become. Okay. Fine. Action is milk out of a rock. You can find God if you look long enough. Nothing gets past time. You've always had too much of it.

Q: Will you confess?

Silence.

Admission is cattle fodder being fed to a war. You need to be small for the big things to exist. Cattle fodder. That is to say. You created a thing for something but you used it for something else anyway. Need is a screaming mistress, as spittle as you want for her to be.

Q: The evidence is incriminating. Will you confess?

Silence.

You can kill a dead thing and have it survive. You can let a live thing live but it still somehow goes and dies. Anything now is an admission of guilt.

Okay. Fine. You can admit this to yourself. A dead fish is a dead fish because you forget to feed it. You've never loved enough. The tarot reader pulls out a wheel of fortune every time you visit. The last time, it was the three of hearts. Okay. Fine. Murder is an ugly thing till you take out its teeth. No snake is worth its body when you pull apart the poison. You are useless if I can live against you.

The fish outside are now alive but

Their spots still match

Who will you match spots with now?

The body of A Dog

For Years, I lived in the body of a dog

Out in a kennel. Punished. Latched to a leash

As if I was on trial for my own death.

[We Can Laugh Over The Irony Later]

Days crack again. Mint dew cascades.

Winter pretending to be summer pretending to be spring.

I learnt to be warm in the summer. The summer when everything
died

And they told us Autumns are sometimes indecisive

Same year I learnt that ethylene is conversive.

That you can die because everyone else is dying.

If All poetry is an act of resistance.

What am I doing here

I outgrow my house to tug

Myself out of this hellhole. I dragged this

Body out of a dying planet to

Create a conversive system.

I laugh. I tug at my fur. I break down the house.

Elegy for Homecoming

The dream flies open like a curtain

I'm on the floor. Delirium and the deluge of home.

Only the worship of Chanel weed floors saying

This womanhood is so divine you had to become an atheist for it

The dream curtains nod and so I must too.

Musk scent. Barrage of grandeur.

The home lilies are trying to

Make it in the industry but

Homegrown is homegrown is home-

Only the unyielding whisper of how

Ferrous sulphate will be green by displacement

There is only place for envy here.

I'm trying to rediscover how sand

Tastes in my mouth but also

How we scraped it off the sandcastles

To try to make a home anyway.

Only the catching flight by its lapels and

Latching one foot to the door to say

High enough. The World is scary but

Mostly that it's not for you.

The dream flutters like a curtain

Or like a butterfly on its last day

Trying to find a resting spot where it can

Be pretty or where the unmourning of it

Doesn't matter but only the yarrows falling.

I try to sit and speak but there's

Only the ask

Coming home and trying to say

This is the world. You'll still have good in it

ode to nameless new spoons

Mother wants to buy new spoons

Outside, the bird song ends, shivering

Reminding me to believe in god

I send out a prayer. God, let me be loved

Got, let me be senseful

And hope that the commonness of it

Makes it comes true.

The more voices, the louder the tragedy

After her, I sit on the balcony

And try to rub off the rust of my

Parent's names together

Off the spoons. Mother's out to buy new

Spoons but she asks if we should get these engraved too

Silver spoons, all lean and tall and seemly

The moon wiggles some light

Into their inevitability. Their ruin.

These are unsalvageable. On the spoons

My parents are together. Mid scrub I stop

The careful edges cut some part of me and

Rust on their name seeps into my skin.

I think of the metaphor & turn off the water.

After You Write

I write "I am the wind" I mean (I love. I long. I yearn)(I cradle
movement)(I'm the silhouette of something)(This purpose is
longitudinal) (The meaning is life, language is parroted) (I am a
bringer of life and betrayer of death) (What I mean is) (I know
language is an attempt at meaning) (What I mean is) (The
movement means only transcendence) (I hold on to your meaning
and I grieve) (Other elements are boring) (I want to live in a
burning house) (I want to keep you alive)

I write "I am an ocean"

Nestled In A Dream, Under the Folds Of Memory

You show up. I watch a movie. I swallow a full bottle of pills. You're at my house. I buy bread. I bake cookies. I go to sleep and I die thrice.

I dream of you — three dreams in a row.

The first, strangled as a grocery store sock set.

You were there and I was mowing grass.

You're holding my hand, and I'm telling you about the story where I dropped the photo frame with my mom's favourite picture. The only copy. Sentimentality ruined her. Preservation was built from the word beg.

I'm telling you about all the scars I have from when I tried to save the picture and how I almost ended up dying.

It's how we found out my body doesn't make enough blood.

The second, I kill myself and I am preserved. The dream buffers.

I'm on the bathroom floor and I'm bleeding out. We all want the same thing.

I'm bleeding out on the bathroom floor and you break down the door.

Your face expresses. I've always taken the front seat for your plays. You've always been at the forefront of mine. You always know what to do. You've been enough people to not be yourself.

Everyone wants this. You get the towel and you get my hand. This is my favourite shade of red. I can never get it right. I should start painting in bathrooms.

"Did you do this to yourself—sweetheart"

I can't bear the sun. Goddamn it sweetheart. Did you cut yourself?

You'd stay as you press the cloth on to my hand.

I've never seen someone as distrustful of a bleeding hand.

You'd think it was the knife.

You always think I do that to myself but no. God hates me as much as you hate knives.

Anyway. You know that story. You find me bleeding and dead. And you mop up the blood.

We don't talk about this. I will forever be in the crevices of this house. I'd like to see you escape me now.

Where did you learn this one? Which play is this from? Did I ever tell you about the story I wrote so you could love me? I gave it to your director. You almost did. You did. I've never been back. I've been bleeding on the bathroom floor and you've been mopping it up all this time.

The third, I spend my summer splitting flowers in the middle. My entire being lurches forward so we can avoid being hit. In this world there are no cars and you still make me jerk forward. You were always special my love.

I'm Madonna. I'm Mary. I'm the whore you asked for.

We go out and we arrange the sticks for a bonfire. I'm arranging it and I'm sorry. I'm sorry I do this. You're pushing me down and you're kissing me and I'm sleeping on fire. That's okay. I would have done that for you. I would have lived in fire if you'd asked me to. Thank you for not asking me to.

Right before I wake up, you punch me and I smile. I've loved your hand since the very first day.

I'm Mary. I'm Madonna. I'm the whore you didn't ask for.

I go to sleep. I swallow a full bottle of pills. I show up at your house. I bake cookies. I buy bread. I watch a movie. I die thrice. You don't show up once.

Inside A Sarcophagus, Steady Tomb

My sister walks with her hands

Crossed over her chest.

Fit to be inside a Sarcophagus.

She's ripe with longing.

I want what's best for her,

Especially when I'm ruining her.

Everything I touch turns to dust.

Then I raised her. We've been doomed from the start.
Fit to be inside a Sarcophagus.

That is to say – She doesn't look dead.

She looks like the coffin.

I am the ruins of everyone I love.

Did you ever wonder if we could get out?

Witness and Victim. We are all bleeding. It all turns to water.

My sister has been dust from the beginning.

Filth raising filth raising filth.

We learnt to build the world

Halfway in the womb. I slept through the last lesson.
We never learned to not abandon it.

Fit to be inside a Sarcophagus.

She will house the body of God within her.

And I'll learn a few prayers.

Local Man Found Pleading To Rock On The Ground. Refuses To Be Separated From It.

Local Man Found Pleading To Rock On The Ground. Refuses To Be Separated From It.

God I am sorry that I abandoned you and called you fake.

God I'm on my knees for you. God can you fix me. God.

I'm sorry. God I'm sorry that I broke down your gates

and tried to prove that you were hell. God I'm sorry

that I fucked up your angel, I thought he was trying

to pick a fight. No one's ever asked me to drink water

before. God, you made me believe that niceness didn't

exist and then let me break into your home and ruin it.

God I know you know what you're doing, why do you do

it anyway? God I swear I'm an angel. God I'm not your

bastard. God you keep screwing me up but I'll forgive you

if you let me back in. God I'm going to dance with your

brother down below. Hell is as real as Heaven is. I've

tasted real. Real tastes like floating into the light but

it's not warm and it's not cold and you're comforted

as you can be. You were born naked, kicking and

screaming, I was born tearing the thumb off of

God's hand. God I promise to sculpt you a new

thumb just let me back in. What would we be if we

Didn't care about being in your home again. God.

Let us in. We promise to be better this time.

I'm an angel which is to say that I stole the wings

Off of one's back. Stole it. I tore it off and let her bleed.

God I've proven my undying loyalty. I've killed for you.

I became an angel and I ate my daughter.

God I'm sorry I showed up with a gun and killed

Five of the women you were being fed by. God I'll

Feed you. Let me back in. Let me back in. Let me back.

God, where would we be if we didn't want to go home again.

God. You're the chef at a popular restaurant

that you've never been able to afford. God emanates

sharpness, strikes. God is guerrilla warfare. God is

allegories beyond human understanding but God is a

human person. God is my human person. God is nothing.

God can I come sit inside you. Just for a little while longer.

Just till I can do this. God. Can I do this?

In A Murder Investigation. You Are —

★ The Victim. You are an ugly ball of longing. You need to be a holy harp head canary eating out of the palm of my hand. You have been demanded. You never make it out of this life because you never made it in this one. You will forever be a twine ball at the top of a hill. You will always be remembered.

★ The Murderer. You are haunted. Your very brick and mortar. The asphalt. There is no tragedy to dictate this horror or justify its existence. There is only purpose or lack thereof. Nothing dead will touch you. Nothing alive will claim you. You will never be wanted. You will always be alone. You will never be someone. You will be haunted. You will be horror. You will be a tragedy.

★ The Investigator. Need is a Parrot that grew up in silence. Need is a parrot that learned to parrot the quiet. Discovery, the final thought. Discovery is a man in a dress that flows enough to be angelic. You can forgive the outfit if it resembles wings. We all want to go back to God. We are all trying to find ways to.

★ The Suspect. You are a bug that lives no longer than a day. It's not even a good day but simply a day although with no frame of reference, you don't know that. I wonder if at the end of my time, my entire life will simply contort itself into a single day without a frame of reference and it will be neither good nor bad. I wish to simply have a day. You are a bug on a bad day and you die a bug on a bad day. Morality is limited to mortality.

★ Judgment Day. Everyone we leave behind. We all mourn the lost however we lose them, for however long. All of us ran to the end. No one is trying to look back. Listen. If you keep looking up you will realise that you are forgiven. The empty forgives the whole. Doesn't even expect the same courtesy. Forgive yourself.

Within Saturn Devoured

I should have jumped rings on Saturn.

I dream of being untouched.

Being untouched in a dream,

My lilies, pure and untouched.

Pure and untouched, but then I wake up.

In the dream, I know how to swim.

Water knows how to swim. I am water.

What do you do after you survive?

After you survive. I jump and I leave.

I hop planets till I am nothing.

I am nothing on Saturn.

Saturn's rings have jumped over me.

Zar.

More than grief.

They call it missionary because

All of this means something Your eyes Feathered and Open

Do you ever think about testimonials and meaning and what all of
this says

About us a butterfly lives its shortest

Life span after the cocoon but wouldn't you rather

Be an ugly and wretched thing

And how you make me want to live for the ugliness

Just so I can have more time with you.

I'm afraid recently more than Ever

But it's in parentheses

[trepidation is a visible grief] [water is a shoreless pit] [a key in the
sand] [what does all of this mean] [where does the lock go] [you
unravel me] [computational logic] [either one is true or none is]
[i'm not religious but you feel like divine intervention] [you make

me feel alive]

Today I feel alive Tomorrow I might convert

Blue orchids bloom into existence inside a book

Explaining the existence of this universe

Your voice makes a nest burrowed in my brain

Like a half intentioned prayer.

A litany of threads is just a necklace

You know enough languages to make me feral

A dead dog will always find its way back home.

Let's pray Let's keep praying I'll get on my knees

And you'll pretend like you aren't God

The Mitral Valve Recognises That A flap Is A Prison

The gospel is a carotid / Weaving between meaning / As above So below / Our flag is a goose trap / but humane / but without the knife / you catch more flies with honey / than with vinegar / but you catch more with blood / If poetry is an attempt at understanding / then what am I doing here? / Rear flash headlights / Reflection is the origin for murder / Sight means conscience / Close your eyes / Night is a cable knit sweater / hanging loose What did the cat and the five year old- / Old story / You give someone a thread / They pull it till it becomes the noose / Who designed the stool? / Triangle's the loneliest shape / If holy makes the blood shed / What makes the blood / Every planet looks / divine from afar / but then we / invent the edge / Eve ate the apple / and / life's been linear since / Hallowed triangulation means / someone always loves someone else / the goose trap means / there's a version of the flag / where two poles find love / and hold on to the third / but there's a reason it's / the myth / What did conscience and guilt have- / Old story / You kill a deer / and all you feel is a jolt / It's so unnecessary / to create a vein that / goes from the heart to the head and not have it / be called / love / or god / or something in between / A peach tree / hits you / and you feel something more than a jolt / linearity means all of this ends /

the goose trap / less humane / more blood / hilt of a dagger / persevering / half dead deer standing behind / the tree / a shard in your head / another in your heart / Close your eyes. What did the jolt and the flag have in common? / Old story / Someone invents a story / Someone else believes all the symbols / while disregarding what they represent.

Reinventing Orpheus - Savitri's Lens

(Self Portrait As The Loved In Every Myth)

This ends badly. The lens is simple. It views

Things only on a 16:9 ratio - the rest

Offering to a dead God. I've been mythologised

In a ratio. You've always lived outside it.

You drag a lion - dead - claw ripped out - blood in hand - and profess -

Here's the good luck - I killed for you - the one where you don't die

Bloody cla(w)uses curdle my stomach . I mutter

Prepositions. In love. On love. Besides love.

The word - a common myth - I try to frame

A memory around the silhouette of your

Chicken fed existence - You - bird metaphors

Crushed against thermal lighting - black then

Blue flitting in the screen - mood lighting

The audience says. I shake. I mutter.

When Orpheus decided to pull me

From the underworld. I remembered nothing

In the elysian except. Joy and how to not

be human. The rest - a long hated memory

No one wants to retrieve. I think of - a lot

But mostly - the shape of heartbeat - across

My wrists and how sleep eludes - grief - and

How I missed - the silhouette of a memory.

After. I remember for a while.

Looking for the light and getting

His face and how I didn't quite

Regret and his name that I don't quite

Remember but it was something like

Notquitelove and then a - memory

No one wants to retrieve. Elysian

Strips human existence to its bare

Essentials. I eat and I move. The grass

Bares its path and is never trodden by

My existence. I move through this world

As weightlessly - as

A crushed bird metaphor.

When Savitri dragged my soul

Over and I came back - I remembered

Everything. Including a weightless

Existence not quite like a crushed

Bird metaphor but more like the trodden

Grass that wants to be trodden. Being

Human isn't all that it's chalked up

To be but the poets have to make

Everything about love. Remember

That butterfly you confessed to

The one who died in your

Book. You said - Hello

Beautiful Thing. I would kill

For you. It's easy to declare

Love with something that makes no

Promises of living but then you

Fought for me to come back and I told

The poets. To wait for sunrise. There's

Always someone you'd turn away from.

You - silhouette of a memory.

I turn back and hold you in my arms.

Acknowledgments

Deep abiding gratitude to my mother, Rishi, Anagha, Erik, Anadya, Shubh, Skye, Kaju, Avi, Argus, Eden, Faiz, Arnav, Dior, Dhwani, Persinaht, Jikan and the other numerous names I've forgotten to mention for their patience and love and support.

Ma, without all the years of you calling me out on surface level metaphors and unitended meaning, this wouldn't exist.

Anadya, without your endless support everytime I sent you a poem simping, these poems would never see the light of the day. Anagha, without your incessant support - asking to keep my poems on your tote bags - I would have never kept writing. Dior, without you saying you want to shit every time you read my poem, my urge to write another glorious poem would never have stood to see the day. Erik, I'm sorry for all that you've heard, if these poems reach someone more viscerally than the rest, this is for you. For Shubh, this title is a quote by you, I hope you turn the page over more than anyone else.

My thanks to Franz Wright, Reyhaneh Jabbari, W. H. Auden, Ali Akbar Sadeghi, Khaled al-Asaad, Carolus Linnaus, Aaron Weiss, Heather Christle, Fanny Howe, Sohrab Sepehri, Lydia Henn, Leslie Jamison, Diane Seuss, Gertrude Stein, Kahlil Gibran, Max Ritvo, Dan Barden, Jericho Brown, Oni Buchanan, Anne Carson, Dhwanee and all other voices in the choir.

An eternity of wild love and gratitude to Orion, who all this is meant to impress. An endless wave of grief and joy, all of this is for you. Endless metaphors as placeholders for you. Grateful for the time you asked me about my love for you. In essence, this entire work is an affirmative to that question.